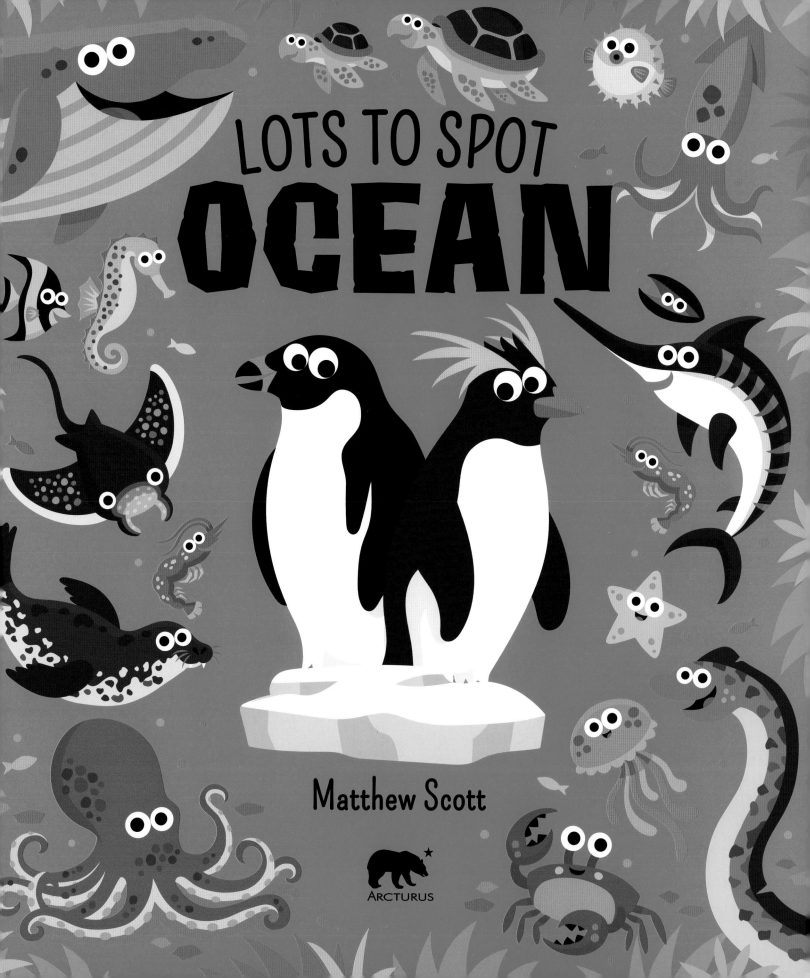

LOTS TO SPOT
OCEAN

Matthew Scott

ARCTURUS

ARCTURUS

This edition published in 2022 by Arcturus Publishing Limited
26/27 Bickels Yard, 151–153 Bermondsey Street,
London SE1 3HA

Illustrated by Matthew Scott
Written by William Potter
Edited by Susannah Bailey
Designed by Trudi Webb

ISBN: 978-1-78428-931-7
CH005491NT
Supplier 29 Date 1022 PI 00003108
Printed in China

CONTENTS

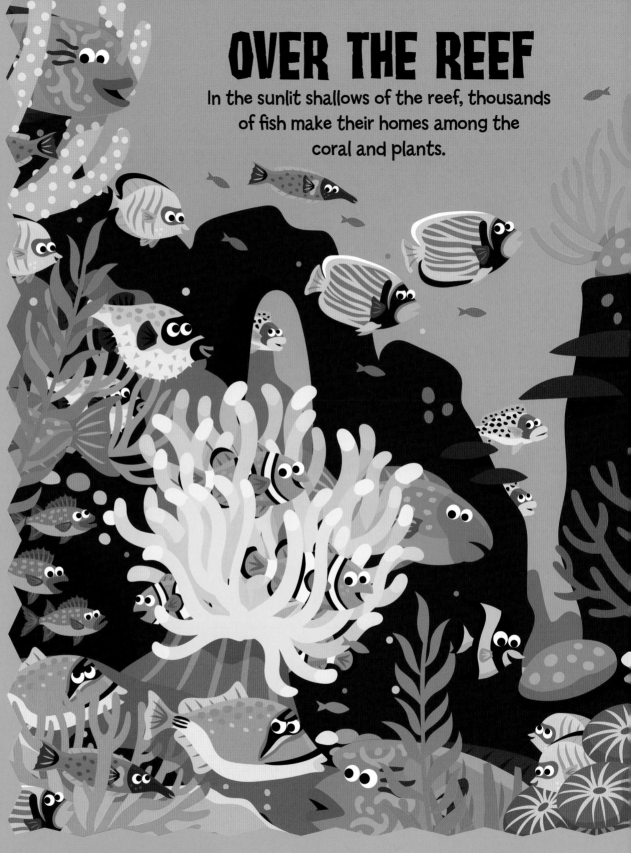

OVER THE REEF

In the sunlit shallows of the reef, thousands of fish make their homes among the coral and plants.

Find 5

Clownfish
Clownfish live among the anemones, but don't feel their stings.

Find 8

Angelfish
Stripy angelfish have tiny mouths that they use to feed on sponges.

Find 9

Sweetlips
Sweetlips are thick-lipped, spotty fish, which swim in large groups called schools.

Find 4

Picasso triggerfish
This bad-tempered fish will chase divers away from its nests.

Find 8

Bird wrasses
Wrasses have long snouts for rooting out tiny shrimp and crabs.

Find 6

Butterflyfish
Yellow butterfly-fish will usually stay in pairs for life.

Find 3

Napoleon wrasses
This bump-headed wrasse can grow to human size. It sleeps in a cave at night.

Find 3

Masked pufferfish
The pufferfish uses the coral as its bed to sleep on at night.

Find 4

Parrotfish
Parrotfish have strong teeth for nibbling coral.

Find 7

Soldierfish
These big-eyed, night-time feeders spend the days hiding in the shadows.

CHILLY NORTH

At the North Pole, animals make their homes on and under the ice in the freezing-cold Arctic waters.

Find 2

Polar bears
Polar bears hunt seals from the ice, but they are also strong swimmers.

Find 11

Arctic chars
When it is time for it to breed, the char's belly turns red.

Find 6

Ribbon seals
Black-and-white ribbon seals have a thick layer of blubber to keep them warm.

Find 8

Narwhals
This unusual whale has a long tooth that grows like a horn on its head.

Find 4

Beluga whales
These whales are also called "sea canaries" for the twittering sound they make.

Find 4

Walruses
Walruses have two long teeth that help them get out of the water, onto the ice.

Find 9

Arctic cod
The Arctic cod has a type of antifreeze in its blood to help it survive the cold.

Find 5

Guillemots
Guillemots dive underwater for several minutes to catch fish.

Find 1

Bowhead whale
This Arctic whale can smash its way through thick ice to breathe.

Find 7

Ringed seals
This is the smallest and also the most common seal in the Arctic.

DARK DEPTHS

The fish that live in the deepest part of the ocean have special ways to find food in the darkness.

Find 3

Anglerfish
Anglerfish use glowing lures on their heads, like fishing rods, to attract food.

Find 3

Pelican eels
Deep-sea pelican eels use their huge mouths like nets to scoop up meals.

Find 4

Deep-sea jellyfish
The jellyfish in the dark depths put on bright light shows.

Find 3

Hagfish
This slimy, eel-like fish can tie itself into a knot.

Find 1

Giant oarfish
The giant oarfish is six times as long as a human adult.

8

Find 5

Black swallowers
With expanding stomachs, these fish can swallow other, much larger fish.

Find 6
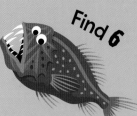

Fangtooth
These small fish have long, sharp fangs, used for gripping food.

Find 3

Vampire squid
The vampire squid isn't a bloodsucker, but it has a dark cloak between its tentacles.

Find 4

Viperfish
These sharp-toothed fish can flash lights in their bodies on and off.

Find 11

Lanternfish
Lanternfish have special organs in their bodies that light up.

9

ROCKY SHORE

The tide washes in and out from the rocky shore twice a day, revealing crabs and shellfish on the sand and stones.

Find 3

Sea stars
If a sea star loses an arm, it can grow it back.

Find 2

Hermit crabs
These small crabs live in shells left behind by other creatures.

Find 4

Common octopuses
The octopus can break open shells with its eight strong arms.

Find 6

Cormorants
Cormorants dry their wings in the sun after diving for fish.

Find 3

Sea scorpions
This camouflaged predator can be mistaken for a rock.

Find 9

Mussels
Mussels live between two shells and glue themselves to rocks using their feet.

Find 3

Common seals
Fish-hunting common seals spend most of their time ashore.

Find 6

Moon jellyfish
This common jellyfish has a bell shape with tiny tentacles around the edge.

Find 6

Common blennies
Blennies can survive out of the water for a short time.

Find 9

Sea urchins
Don't touch! This slow-moving creature grows a shell with sharp spines.

Find 6

Lionfish
Beware this stripy fish's spines—they are very poisonous!

Find 8

Redcoat squirrelfish
This fish has a spiky fin along its back and large eyes for finding food at night.

Find 6

Scuba divers
Divers breathe air from a tank so they can swim deep under water.

ANCIENT SHIPWRECK

A sunken ship is rusting on the sea bed. It is now a home for corals and fish, and a great place for divers to explore.

Find 7

Spadefish
These fish have big, flat bodies. They often swim in large schools.

Find 12

Bluestripe snappers
Bright bluestripe snappers like to swim around corals in groups.

Find 3

Moray eels
Moray eels are snakelike fish with many tiny teeth. They like to hide in the rocks.

Find 4

Devil scorpionfish
This poisonous fish hides in the sand and shuffles along on two side fins.

Find 9

Bannerfish
The bannerfish was named after the long fin on its back.

Find 6

Bluefin trevallies
These strong swimmers will chase and catch much smaller fish.

Find 5

Coral groupers
This big, spotty fish feeds on crab, octopus, and squid.

13

Find 4

Mako sharks
The fastest of the sharks, the mako can reach up to 90kph (56mph).

Find 3

John dory
The john dory has long fins and a large spot on its side.

Find 6

Marblefish
Camouflaged marblefish keep the seaweed trim by nibbling it.

Find 2

KELP FOREST
Kelp is a large seaweed. It may grow to form an underwater forest where sea creatures can nest and graze.

Stingrays
Stingrays have spines on their tails that can give you a deadly sting.

Find 4

Red pigfish
Male pigfish grow almost twice as big as the females.

Find 5

Porcupine fish

When in danger, this fish can puff itself up like a spiky balloon.

Find 3

Common triplefins

This tiny fish was named for the three fins on its back.

Find 6

Blue maomaos

Bright blue maomaos swim in large groups near the surface.

Find 7

Yellowtail kingfish

This fast-swimming fish is a prized catch for fishermen.

Find 3

Spotted black groupers

These large fish may live all of their lives in the same part of a reef.

MANGROVE MAZE

Mangroves are trees that can grow in salty water by the coast. Their underwater roots are a shelter and nursery for young fish.

Find 2

Saltwater crocodiles
The largest reptile on earth will eat almost anything that comes close— including people!

Find 5

Yellow sea horses
Sea horses grip on to the mangrove roots with their tails.

Find 8

Mud crabs
When the water level is low, this crab moves into a burrow or muddy hole.

Find 17

Anchovies
Anchovies are small fish that are often hunted by larger fish.

Find 7

Mudskippers
This fish can survive out of the water, where it uses its fins to flop about.

Find 6

Banded archerfish
Archerfish will spit at insects to knock them into the water.

Find 4

Mangrove jacks
This hunter will hide in the mangrove roots to surprise passing fish and crabs.

Find 7

Cardinalfish
The male keeps his young safe by carrying them in his mouth.

Find 8

Mullets
Mullets swim near the water's surface, picking at tiny pieces of food.

Find 6

Combtooth blennies
This small, shy fish has two long fins, like combs, on its back.

17

Long ago, this city was flooded by the ocean. Its ruins and ancient treasures are now a habitat for plants and fish.

Find 14

Zebra sea breams
The stripy sea bream feeds on small shellfish, worms, and urchins.

Find 5

White-spotted octopuses
When disturbed, this octopus turns a bright red.

Find 7

Dogfish
The dogfish is a type of shark. It has rough skin, like sandpaper.

Find 5

Cornetfish
This long, pipe-like fish can detect prey using its sensitive tail.

Find 4

Eagle rays
The ray has a flat body, with large fins and a mouth on its underside.

Bearded fireworms
This centipede-like creature can give a nasty sting through its bristles.

Red sea stars
These distinctive starfish are bright scarlet!

Sea hares
The sea hare is a large underwater slug that feeds on seaweed.

Find **8**

Find **4**

Find **3**

Find **3**

Stargazers
This fish buries itself in the sandy sea bed, ready to lunge at small prey.

Find **5**

Sea potatoes
This is not a vegetable—it's a spiny urchin that burrows into the sandy bed.

NIGHT DIVE

Night time is when many fish choose to hunt.
Soft corals appear and tiny creatures leave their hideouts.

Find 10

Cleaner shrimp
Banded shrimp use their claws to remove bugs from passing fish.

Find 3

Decorator crabs
This crab sticks objects to bristles on its back to camouflage itself.

Find 4

Sea kraits
These highly venomous snakes hunt under rocks for eels and small fish.

Find 15

Polyps
Polyps are tiny animals that connect together to form coral reefs.

Find 5

Epaulette sharks
This small, spotty, crab-eating shark is harmless to humans.

Find **5**

Cuttlefish
Cuttlefish are brainy relatives of squid that signal by changing their skin tones.

Find **3**

Crown-of-thorns starfish
This huge, poisonous sea star eats coral and destroys reefs.

Find **2**

Slipper lobsters
Slipper lobsters have flat feelers on their heads, like plates.

Find **6**

Blackspotted puffers
To defend itself, the puffer can swell up with water.

Find **2**

Pineapple sea cucumbers
This sea star relative can squirt out its own guts if attacked!

21

SANDY SEA BED

The North Atlantic ocean is home to many fish. Flatfish rest on the sea bed or burrow into the sand. Their skin patterns help them to hide.

Find 8

Clams
These shelled creatures can live for hundreds of years.

Find 4

Lobsters
The American lobster can weigh as much as a five-year-old child.

Find 5

Skates
These flatfish spend most of their time buried in the sand.

Find 4

Horseshoe crabs
This living fossil is more closely related to a spider than a crab.

Find 12

Haddocks
A female haddock can produce up to three million eggs in a year.

Find 4

Flounders
This flatfish has both eyes on one side of its body.

Find 6

Scallops
Scallops open and close their shells to swim through the water.

Find 3

Red gurnards
This bottom-dwelling fish has fins that open out like wings.

Find 3

Oyster toadfish
Toadfish use camouflage to catch other fish by surprise.

Find 15

Herrings
The herring is one of the world's most common fish.

Large fish patrol the edge of the coral reef where it meets the deep blue ocean. They graze on plants or hunt for prey.

Find 4

Unicornfish
The thin-bodied unicornfish has a long bump on its head, like a horn.

Find 7

Pipefish
The pipefish is a relative of the sea horse and has a tube-like snout and a tiny mouth.

Find 16

Pyramid butterflyfish
This fish swims to open water to feed on the plankton it finds there.

Find 12

Sponges
A sponge is an animal with holes that water can pass through.

Find 3

White-tip reef sharks
This night-hunting shark rarely threatens people.

Find 9

Green sea turtles
Female sea turtles swim back to the beach of their birth to lay their eggs.

Find 12

Blackfin barracudas
Barracudas are fast-moving predators with sharp teeth.

Find 3

Leaffish
The poisonous leaffish pretends to be a leaf lying in the water.

Find 5

Bigeye trevallies
Trevallies spend the day in a large group before hunting at night.

Find 8

Yellowfin tuna
This large but fast fish has long, curved, yellow fins.

25

VOLCANIC VENTS

In the deepest parts of the ocean, boiling hot water bursts out of cracks in the earth's surface. By these vents, strange, pale creatures survive in the dark.

Find 4

Deepsea vent octopuses

This octopus uses its arms to feel its way around in the dark.

Find 7

Scale worms

These flat creatures are covered in scales to defend themselves.

Find 5

Vent crabs

In the darkness, this white crab has to use special night vision to see.

Find 12

Limpets

Limpets are relatives of the snail. They are often found sticking to rocks.

Find 13

Clams

These clams live along the vents where boiling liquid pours out.

Find 4

Pompeii worms

Pompeii worms have feather-shaped heads and bristly bodies.

Find 3

Squat lobsters

This small, flat, prickly lobster feeds on tiny bacteria living around the vents.

Find 4

Eelpout fish

The eelpout fish wriggles between tube worms, hunting limpets and snails.

Find 10

Vent shrimp

Tiny vent shrimp have no need for eyes in the darkness.

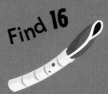

Find 16

Giant tube worms

This large worm takes in chemicals through the red part of its body.

In the warm, blue waters of an Australian marine park, giants of the ocean gather in large numbers.

Find 4

Hawksbill turtles
These turtles have sharp beaks used for biting jellyfish and sponges.

Find 7

Bottlenose dolphins
Playful bottlenose dolphins like to stay in their family group.

Find 4

Dugongs
This marine mammal grazes on seagrass like a cow.

Find 10

Remoras
This suckerfish sticks to large fish, such as rays and sharks.

Find 1

Whale sharks
Whale sharks are the world's largest fish, but they only eat tiny fish and plankton.

Manta rays
The largest of the rays uses its fins like wings to glide through the water.

Find 3

Find 13

Spangled emperors
These golden fish turn stripy when they are frightened.

Find 5

Loggerhead turtles
Loggerheads can hold their breath for up to four hours.

Find 10

Mahi-mahis
Mahi-mahis grow into adults in just five months.

Find 13

Spanish mackerels
These fast-swimming fish lay eggs that float on the water's surface.

FEEDING FRENZY

When large schools of sardines gather, sharks, dolphins, and other marine creatures arrive to enjoy the feast.

Find 4

Blacktip sharks
These sharks are regularly spotted by divers.

Find 7

Cape fur seals
The large cape fur seal twists and turns in the water.

Find 8

African penguins
These penguins live on the warm African coast and go diving for fish.

Find 12

Common dolphins
The dolphin works in a team, herding the sardines into a large ball.

Find 2

Humpback whales
Male humpbacks are known for their songs, which can last up to 15 minutes at a time.

Hammerhead sharks

This strange shark has its eyes at the ends of its odd-shaped head.

Find 7

Cape gannets

These large seabirds nest on the coast and dive for fish.

Find 3

Copper sharks

Copper sharks take turns to swim into the sardines and take bites of them.

Find 1

Bryde's whale

Bryde's whale can swallow a shoal of sardines with one big mouthful.

Find 13

Garricks

This large predator hunts smaller fish, such as the sardine.

CORAL CLOSE UP

You have to look very carefully to see these tiny creatures living on and around the coral and plants on the reef.

Find 2

Spiny devilfish
This camouflaged fish hides venomous spines on its back.

Find 4

Mimic octopuses
Clever mimic octopuses change their skin tone to copy animals and plants.

Find 3

Tassled frogfish
This fish's tassels make it hard to spot in the seaweed.

Find 14

Cleaner wrasses
Cleaner wrasses peck away dead skin from visiting fish.

Find 2

Lizardfish
Lizardfish tend to swim in sandy or muddy areas.

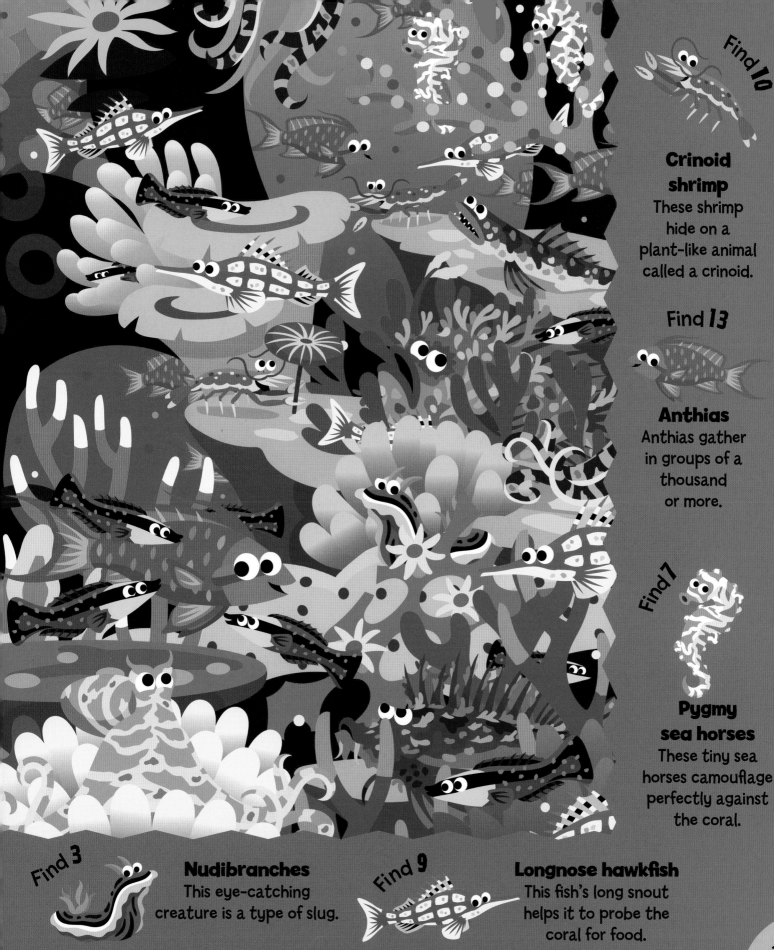

Find 10

Crinoid shrimp
These shrimp hide on a plant-like animal called a crinoid.

Find 13

Anthias
Anthias gather in groups of a thousand or more.

Find 7

Pygmy sea horses
These tiny sea horses camouflage perfectly against the coral.

Find 3

Nudibranches
This eye-catching creature is a type of slug.

Find 9

Longnose hawkfish
This fish's long snout helps it to probe the coral for food.

33

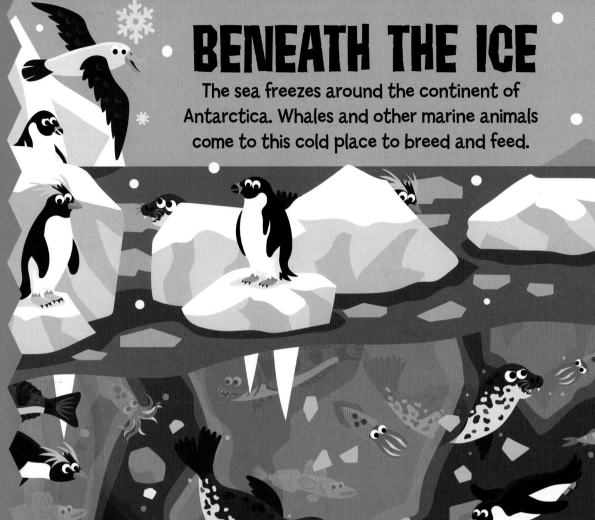

BENEATH THE ICE

The sea freezes around the continent of Antarctica. Whales and other marine animals come to this cold place to breed and feed.

Find 3

Orca whales

These killer whales hunt like wolves, in a group called a pod.

Find 8

Leopard seals

This lone hunter will swim after penguins in the water.

Find 10

Rockhopper penguins

Rockhoppers have spiky feathers on their heads.

Find 12

Squid

Most squid are small, but some deep-sea squid grow as long as buses!

Find 7

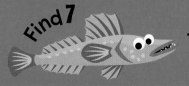

Icefish

This strange fish has clear blood, which isn't red.

Find 7

King penguins
These large penguins can dive deep underwater to catch fish and squid.

Find 1

Blue whale
This is the largest animal that has ever lived on earth.

Find 5

Adélie penguins
Young adélie penguins first enter the water at two months old.

Find 6

Antarctic toothfish
These predators can hunt in extremely cold water.

Find 4

Albatrosses
Each wing on an albatross is as long as a human adult.

NAUTICAL NUMBERS

There are four different kinds of fish in these waters, but which one is there most of?

MAPPING THE OCEAN

Where does each small square go in the grid? Write the numbers in the correct squares to complete the picture.

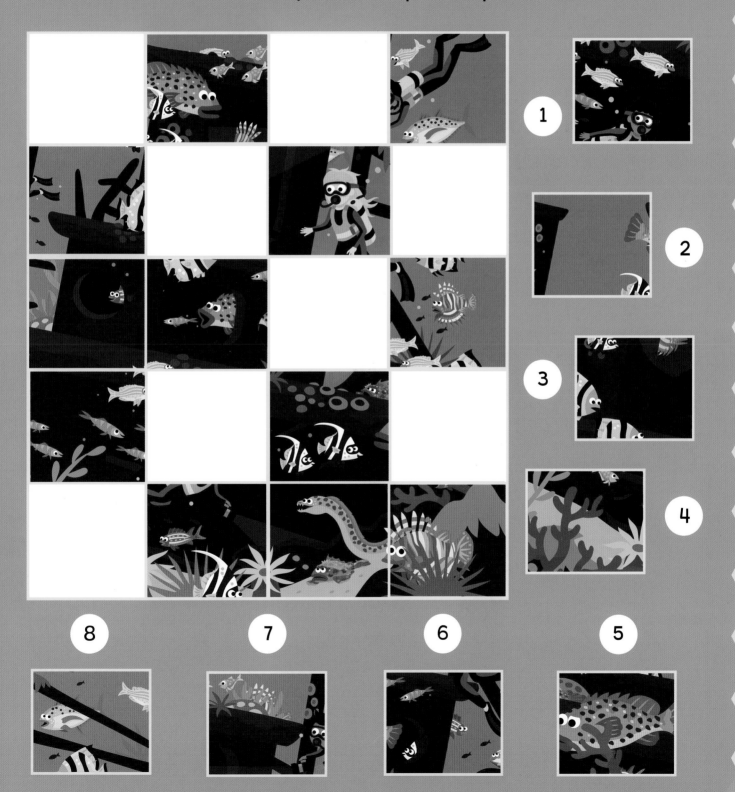

CAUGHT OUT

Help the fish escape through the holes in the fishing net to reach its friends.

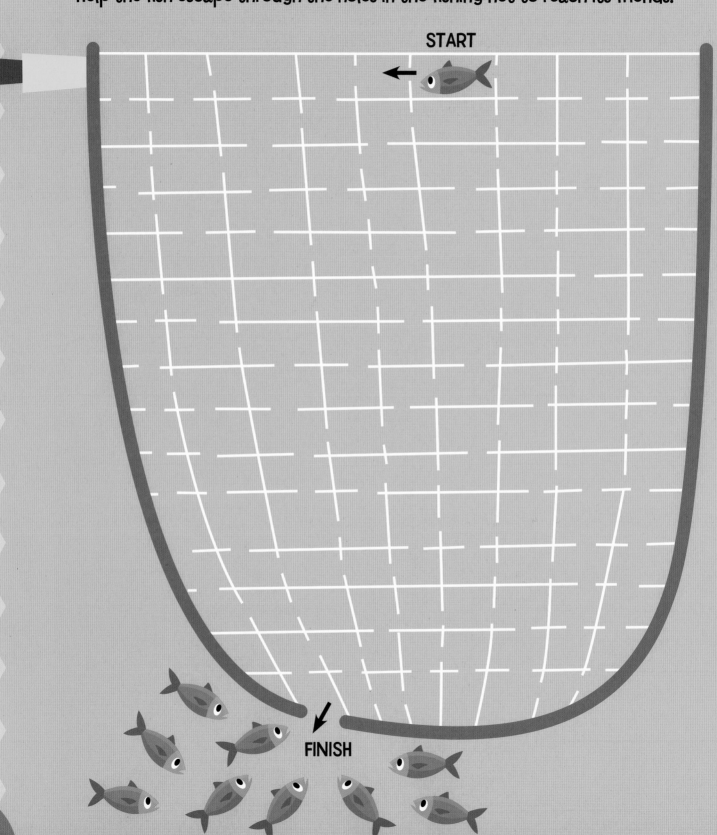

START

FINISH

SINGLE STAR

Sort these stars into matching pairs.
Which one is the odd star out?

FIT THE FISH

Where are the close-up details in this undersea scene?

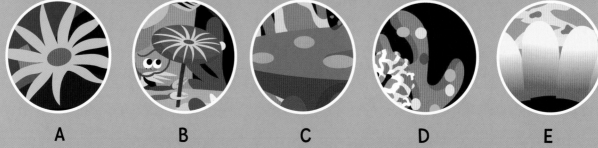

A   B   C   D   E

SEA SHADOWS

Which fish have divers found at the bottom of the sea?

ANSWERS

4–5 OVER THE REEF

- Clownfish
- Angelfish
- Sweetlips
- Picasso triggerfish
- Bird wrasses
- Parrotfish
- Soldierfish
- Masked pufferfish
- Napoloeon wrasses
- Butterflyfish

6–7 CHILLY NORTH

- Polar bears
- Arctic chars
- Ribbon seals
- Narwhals
- Beluga whales
- Bowhead whale
- Ringed seals
- Guillemots
- Arctic cod
- Walruses

8–9 DARK DEPTHS

- Anglerfish
- Pelican eels
- Deep-sea jellyfish
- Hagfish
- Giant oarfish
- Viperfish
- Lanternfish
- Vampire squid
- Fangtooth
- Black swallowers

ANSWERS

10–11 ROCKY SHORE

- Sea stars
- Hermit crabs
- Common octopuses
- Cormorants
- Sea scorpions
- Common blennies
- Sea urchins
- Moon jellyfish
- Common seals
- Mussels

12–13 ANCIENT SHIPWRECK

- Lionfish
- Redcoat squirrelfish
- Scuba divers
- Spadefish
- Bluestripe snappers
- Bluefin trevallies
- Coral groupers
- Bannerfish
- Devil scorpionfish
- Moray eels

14–15 KELP FOREST

- Mako sharks
- John dory
- Marblefish
- Stingrays
- Red pigfish
- Yellowtail kingfish
- Spotted black groupers
- Blue maomaos
- Common triplefins
- Porcupine fish

ANSWERS

16–17 MANGROVE MAZE

- Saltwater crocodiles
- Yellow sea horses
- Mud crabs
- Anchovies
- Mudskippers
- Mullets
- Combtooth blennies
- Cardinalfish
- Mangrove jacks
- Banded archerfish

18–19 SUNKEN CITY

- Zebra sea breams
- White-spotted octopuses
- Dogfish
- Cornetfish
- Eagle rays
- Stargazers
- Sea potatoes
- Sea hares
- Red sea stars
- Bearded fireworms

20–21 NIGHT DIVE

- Cleaner shrimp
- Decorator crabs
- Sea kraits
- Polyps
- Epaulette sharks
- Blackspotted puffers
- Pineapple sea cucumbers
- Slipper lobsters
- Crown-of-thorns starfish
- Cuttlefish

ANSWERS

22–23 SANDY SEA BED

- Clams
- Lobsters
- Skates
- Horseshoe crabs
- Haddocks
- Oyster toadfish
- Herrings
- Red gurnards
- Scallops
- Flounders

24–25 THE DROP OFF

- Unicornfish
- Pipefish
- Pyramid butterflyfish
- Sponges
- White-tip reef sharks
- Bigeye trevallies
- Yellowfin tuna
- Leaffish
- Blackfin barracudas
- Green sea turtles

26–27 VOLCANIC VENTS

- Deepsea vent octopuses
- Scale worms
- Vent crabs
- Limpets
- Clams
- Vent shrimp
- Giant tube worms
- Eelpout fish
- Squat lobsters
- Pompeii worms

ANSWERS

28–29 GENTLE GIANTS

- Hawksbill turtles
- Bottlenose dolphins
- Dugongs
- Remoras
- Whale sharks
- Mahi-mahis
- Spanish mackerels
- Loggerhead turtles
- Spangled emperors
- Manta rays

30–31 FEEDING FRENZY

- Blacktip sharks
- Cape fur seals
- African penguins
- Common dolphins
- Humpback whales
- Bryde's whale
- Garricks
- Copper sharks
- Cape gannets
- Hammerhead sharks

32–33 CORAL CLOSE UP

- Spiny devilfish
- Mimic octopuses
- Tassled frogfish
- Cleaner wrasses
- Lizardfish
- Nudibranches
- Longnose hawkfish
- Pygmy sea horses
- Anthias
- Crinoid shrimps

ANSWERS

34–35 BENEATH THE ICE

- Orca whales
- Leopard seals
- Rockhopper penguins
- Squid
- Icefish
- Antarctic toothfish
- Albatrosses
- Adélie penguins
- Blue whale
- King penguins

36 NAUTICAL NUMBERS

There are 20 of these fish.

There are only 16 each of all the other fish.

37 MAPPING THE OCEAN

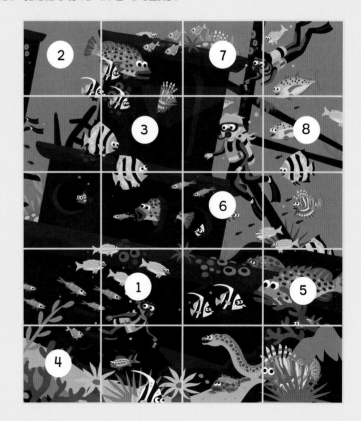

ANSWERS

38 CAUGHT OUT

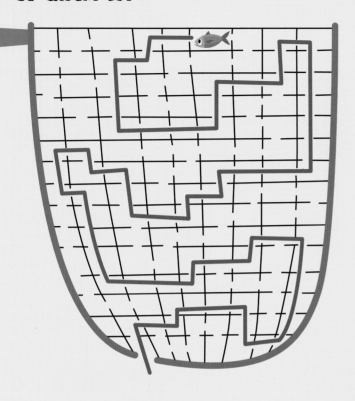

39 SINGLE STAR

40 FIT THE FISH

41 SEA SHADOWS